VERBAL REASONING
TECHNIQUE AND PRACTICE 4

Susan J. Daughtrey M.Ed

Childs World Education Limited
1993

ACKNOWLEDGEMENTS

I would like to thank my husband Brian without whose patient support and encouragement this series of books would not have been written. I must also express my thanks to our children Sara and James who enthusiastically contributed many ideas and performed numerous practical exercises. And finally, a special thanks to my students who (often unknowingly) provided the inspiration and feedback which has been so encouraging.

Brancaster, Norfolk.
1993.

ISBN 1 898696 78 0

Childs World Education Limited
PO Box 1881, Gerrards Cross,
Buckinghamshire SL9 9AN England

Printed in Great Britain by Halstan & Co. Ltd., Amersham, Bucks.

First published 1993.
First edition 1993.
Reprinted 1994, 1995, 1996, 1998, 1999 (twice), 2000, 2001.

© 1993 Susan J. Daughtrey M.Ed.

TECHNIQUE TYPE THIRTY-ONE

In these questions you are asked to identify the only statement that must be true based on information given.

Example:
If E6 washing powder is bigger than size E3 but smaller than E15 then underline the ONE statement below that must be true:

a.   Size E6 is the biggest of all three.
b.   Size E3 must be very small.
c.   Size E15 powder is the smallest of all three.
d.   Size E6 powder is bigger than size E3 powder.

Technique:

1.   You must concentrate only on the information given.
Do not allow any other facts you know about the subject to influence your decision.

2.   If possible, draw a diagram to help sort out the information.
An 'arrow' sketch here may help.   Answer: *d*

NOTE:
If there is a word such as 'usually', 'frequently', 'might' or 'could' in the information given, you cannot be absolutely certain that something happened. Here, for instance:

Susan USUALLY goes roller skating on Saturday evenings. Tomorrow is Sunday. Underline one of the following statements which MUST be true:

a.   Yesterday was Friday.
b.   Yesterday was Saturday.
c.   Susan went skating today.
d.   Susan went roller skating yesterday.

Certainly yesterday was not Saturday, nor did Susan go skating yesterday.
You cannot even be certain Susan went roller skating today because whilst she USUALLY does, it is not certain that today she did! Indeed, the only thing you can be certain about is that yesterday was Friday.
The correct answer is therefore *a.*

Example:
James' brother USUALLY brings presents for him on his return from holiday. He is returning from holiday today, so . . .

a.   James' brother will have presents with him.
b.   He will have no presents with him.
c.   He is likely to have presents with him.
d.   James is excited.

Perhaps James is excited, but it says nothing about this in the information, so do not be distracted. It says the brother USUALLY brings presents for James so it is not true to say he will have NO presents with him, nor is it true to say he will certainly have presents with him. The only thing you can say with certainty is he is LIKELY to have presents with him. This is the only statement here that is TRUE. Here then the answer would be *c*.

Remember: You are looking for the only statement you can be certain about. There is always one.

You are allowed 30 seconds per question.

Now turn to the next page for Practice of this Type.

PRACTICE TYPE THIRTY-ONE

Henry II died in 1189 the same year as Richard I came to the throne. Richard reigned for 10 years. Now underline ONE of the following answers which must be true:

    a.   Henry II died in 1199.

    b.   Richard ruled for longer than Henry II.

    c.   Richard came to the throne in 1189.

    d.   Richard I died in 1189.

Sara usually goes to Girl Guides on a Thursday. Today is Wednesday. Now underline the ONE answer below which must be true:

    a.   Sara went to Girl Guides today.

    b.   Sara went to Girl Guides yesterday.

    c.   Tomorrow Sara will go to Girl Guides.

    d.   Tomorrow will be Thursday.

If remote-controlled cars are more expensive than mechanical cars and radio-controlled cars are more expensive than remote-controlled cars, underline only ONE of the following statements that must be true:

    a.   James enjoys playing with his remote-controlled car.

    b.   Mechanical cars are more expensive than remote-controlled cars.

    c.   Radio-controlled cars are cheaper than remote-controlled cars.

    d.   Radio-controlled cars are the most expensive.

Liam and Luke were absent from school last week. Luke had four days off. Liam had three days off. Now underline the ONE answer that must be true:

    a.   Both boys were ill for the first three days of the week.

    b.   Both boys were absent together for at least two days.

    c.   Both boys missed soccer on Monday.

    d.   Both boys were off school for 7 days.

Jenny and Jessica have short hair. Nicky and Jade have long hair. Jade, Jenny and Nicky are tall. Jessica is not. Jade does not wear spectacles, the others do. Now underline the ONE statement below which must be true:

    a.   Jade and Jenny are tall and have long hair.

    b.   Jenny and Jessica have short hair and are tall.

    c.   Jessica and Jenny have short hair and wear spectacles.

    d.   Jessica and Nicky wear spectacles and have short hair.

Christmas Day is on Friday. Three days after tomorrow is Christmas Day. Now underline the ONE statement below which must be true:

    a.   Today is Sunday.

    b.   The day before yesterday was Saturday.

    c.   Tomorrow is Wednesday.

    d.   Shaun is excited.

Black sports cars go faster than blue saloon cars but slower than red sports cars. Now underline the ONE statement below which must be true:

    a.   Black sports cars go very fast.

    b.   Blue saloon cars are the slowest.

    c.   Red sports cars go slower than blue saloon cars.

    d.   Black sports cars go slower than blue saloon cars.

James and Tom like rugby. Tim and Nicholas prefer football. Only Nicholas does not enjoy roller skating. Now underline the ONE statement below which must be true:

    a.   James and Tim like roller skating but not rugby.

    b.   Nicholas and Tim prefer football and roller skating.

    c.   Tom does not enjoy football or roller skating.

    d.   James and Tom enjoy rugby and roller skating.

TECHNIQUE TYPE THIRTY-TWO

On Verbal Reasoning papers, there are FOUR different Types of code question that can be asked. I shall deal with each Type separately (Types Thirty-Two to Thirty-Five). This first Type, Type Thirty-Two, is the most difficult.

Within Type Thirty-Two, four different Kinds of code question can be identified (32.1, 32.2, 32.3, 32.4). I am going to explain how to do each Kind individually. But first of all, let us consider the LAYOUT of each of these Kinds of question. This remains the same.

TYPE 32.1:

Example One:

   If L E A F is written Q I D H how would you write the code word for T R E E?

LAYOUT:

Here you are asked for a CODE answer so set your working out with the WORD on top. Like this:

word	L	E	A	F
code	Q	I	D	H

Example Two:

        If V X Q stands for S U N what does K R W stand for?

LAYOUT:

Here you are asked for a WORD answer so set your working out with the CODE on top. Like this:

code	V	X	Q
word	S	U	N

Technique:

When you have set one on top of the other, working from the top row to the bottom row (I shall now refer to question Example One above):

1.   Ask: How has the L   become a   Q ?
             How has the E   become an   I ?
             How has the A   become a   D ?
             How has the F   become an   H ?

In this Type of code question you are always given an alphabet to assist you. Look at the alphabet to help you decide.

A B C D E F G H I J K L M N O P Q R S T U V W X Y Z

2.   Counting forwards (towards Z) or backwards (towards A), record what is happening underneath the letters.

> L has moved forward 5 places to Q   (+5)
> E has moved forward 4 places to I   (+4)
> A has moved forward 3 places to D   (+3)
> F has moved forward 2 places to H   (+2)

+5 means the letter has moved towards Z five places. (–2 would mean the letter had moved back two places towards A.)

word	L	E	A	F
	----------------------			
code	Q	I	D	H
	+5	+4	+3	+2

3.   Now rewrite what is happening underneath the code/word you are asked to solve.   Like this:

word	T	R	E	E

	+5	+4	+3	+2

4.   Calculate your answer.

> Start at T and count forward 5 letters   (Y)
> Start at R and count forward 4 letters   (V)
> Start at E and count forward 3 letters   (H)
> Start at E and count forward 2 letters   (G)

Answer: The CODE for tree is *Y V H G*

NOTE:

1. If you are asked for a WORD answer, be sure your answer is a sensible word. If it is not you have probably made a mistake. GO BACK AND CHECK.

2. If the second word/code has more/less letters than the first word/code, continue the pattern for the number of letters given, like this:

If S O O N can be written R M L J in code, how would you write S U N N Y?

word	S	O	O	N		S	U	N	N	Y
	----------------------					------------------------------				
code	R	M	L	J		–1	–2	–3	–4	–5
	–1	–2	–3	–4		R	S	K	J	T

Answer: *R S K J T*

TYPE 32.2:

Example:

> If Y V W is the code for B E D what is the code word for C O T ?

Technique:

1.   Try working in from each end of the alphabet to help you like this:

This is a much quicker way than writing a reverse alphabet under the first alphabet. That method is using up valuable time!

2.   Solution:

word	B E D	C O T
code	Y V W	
Position of letters:	2 5 4	3 15 20

3.   C is the 3rd letter from the beginning of the alphabet.
This matches with X - the third letter from the end of the alphabet.
In this way, calculate your answer.   Answer: *X L G*

TYPE 32.3:

Example:

> If 2 1 14 11 is the code for B A N K what is the code for B O O K ?

Technique:

Give each letter of the alphabet a number.
If B is the 2nd letter, A is the 1st letter, N is the 14th letter and K is the 11th letter, what are the positions of the letters of the word B O O K ?

B is 2   O is 15   and   K is 11   Answer: *2 15 15 11*

Sometimes there can be a mixture of Kind 32.1 and Kind 32.3 where you need to combine the two Techniques:

Example:

  If 13 P 15 O is the code for M O O N what is the code for S H O E ?

Technique:

word	M O O N	S H O E
code	13 P 15 O	✓ +1 ✓ +1
	✓ +1 ✓ +1	19 I 15 F

Answer: *19   I   15   F*

NOTE:

It is a good idea if you can memorise the position of some of the letters in the alphabet. For example know:

E	is the 5th letter
M	is the 13th letter
T	(for 20) is the 20th letter

Using these as starting points will be quicker to calculate for example, the 19th letter, the 15th, and so on, without having to start at A each time.

TYPE 32.4:

Example:

  If C A A B T C means C A T what does D A O B G C mean ?

Technique:

Here the code word has been 'expanded' - other letters have been inserted to disguise the real word.

    C a A b T c = C A T   D a O b G c = D O G
      ^   ^   ^   ^   ^   ^

  You are allowed 30 seconds per question.

  Now turn to the next page for Practice of these Types.

PRACTICE TYPE THIRTY-TWO

A B C D E F G H I J K L M N O P Q R S T U V W X Y Z

The above alphabet will help you to find the answers to the following code questions. Write your answers in the brackets.

Example TYPE 32.1:

If L E A F is written Q I D H what would be the code word for T R E E?
Write your answer in the brackets. . . . . (__*YVHG*__)

Now try these:

If K V N Q means J U M P then T U P Q means . . . . (_____)

If P I N E is written N G L C then C O N E is written . . . . (_____)

If P E N C I L is written K A K A H L then R U L E R is written (_____)

If H H T D means F I R E then H K C L G means . . . . (_____)

If H P Q Q V means F R O S T then H G U F means . . . . (_____)

If C N D G F means B L A C K then H T H I I means . . . . (_____)

If S O C K is written O L A J then F O O T is written . . . . (_____)

If G A M E is written K D O F then P A C K is written . . . . (_____)

Example TYPE 32.2:

If Y V W stands for B E D then X L G stands for . . . . (__*COT*__)

Now try these:

If U Z W means F A D then S Z G V means . . . . (_____)

If X Z I means C A R then E Z M means . . . . (_____)

If D E S K is written W V H P then B O O K is written . . . . (_____)

If F A D E is written U Z W V then S T A G E is written . . . . . (_____)

If T F M means G U N then S R G means . . . . (_____)

If B O X is written Y L C then L I D is written . . . . (_____)

If X F G means C U T then S F I G means . . . . (_____)

If F R O M is written U I L N then W I T H is written . . . . (_____)

A B C D E F G H I J K L M N O P Q R S T U V W X Y Z

Example TYPE 32.3:

If 2 1 14 11 means B A N K then 2 15 15 11 means (_B O O K_)

Now try these:

If 8 1 20 means H A T then 13 1 14 means . . . . (_____)

If 20 18 5 5 means T R E E then 12 5 1 6 means . . . . (_____)

If C A S E is written 4 2 20 6 then T R U N K is written . . . . (_____)

If O C E A N is written L 4 B 2 K then R I V E R is written . . . (_____)

If P A P E R is written M 2 S 6 O then F O L D E R is written . (_____)

If 3 B 7 F means C A G E then 4 F 1 S means . . . . (_____)

If 3 M 1 R means C O A T then 2 M 15 R means . . . . (_____)

If S A N D is written V 1 Q 4 then W A T E R is written. . . . . . (_____)

Example TYPE 32.4:

If S A I B T C stands for S I T then C A U B P C stands for . . . (__C U P_)

Now try these:

If H A A B T C means H A T then H A E B A C D D means . . . (_____)

If S T O P is written S S T O O P then W A I T is written . . . . . (_____)

If M O A N is written N N A O M M then D A R E is written . (_____)

If V A S E is written V A A S E E then S T E M is written . . . . (_____)

If B A I B T C means B I T then F A E B D C means . . . . (_____)

If C X O Y D Z means C O D then R X O Y E Z means . . . . (_____)

If P P E E N N means P E N then P P I I G G means . . . . (_____)

If B O Y is written B B O Y Y then C A T is written . . . . (_____)

TYPES 32.1 to 32.4:

A B C D E F G H I J K L M N O P Q R S T U V W X Y Z

The above alphabet will help you to find the answers to the following code questions. Write your answers in the brackets.

If Y L B means B O Y then T R I O means . . . . (_____)

If I I V M means D E S K then W Y O G S means . . . . (_____)

If B R O O M is written 2 U 15 L 13 then D U S T is written . . . . (_____)

If C A T is written B B Z S S then D O G is written . . . . (_____)

If M A I D is written M X A Y I Z D then T R A Y is written . . . . (_____)

If F C T E means C A S E then S C D K means . . . . (_____)

If X S Z R I means C H A I R then Y V M X S means . . . . (_____)

If R 4 I 16 N 13 means S C H O O L then P I T C H is written . . (_____)

If S H I P is written S A H B I C P then Y A C H T is written . . . (_____)

If C R O W is written X I L D then N E S T is written . . . . (_____)

If S T A N D is T V D R Y then T V L P G is . . . . (_____)

If M O O N is N L L M then X O L F W is . . . . (_____)

If 22 9 12 12 1 means V I L L A then O L I V E is written . . . . . . (_____)

If P L A T E is written J Q W W C then S P O O N is . . . . (_____)

If C M U N P O means C U P the M M U N G O means . . . . (_____)

If U R H S means F I S H then Y R I W means . . . . (_____)

If H E A D is written H A E B A C D D then F A C E is written . (_____)

If B I R D is written 4 K 20 F then C A G E is written . . . . (_____)

If P A W is written K Z D then H O O F is written . . . . (_____)

If I X J S means L A M P then Y R I E means . . . . (_____)

TECHNIQUE TYPE THIRTY-THREE

This is the second Type of code question in this book. Within this category two Kinds can be identified.

TYPE 33.1:

Here we are trying to match numbers to words. Once achieved, words can be written in number code, and number code translated into words.

Example:

5681, 5762, 5761, 8651 and 7651 are codes for the words HOSE, SHOE, ROSE, SORE and SHOW but not in that order. Find the code for each of the following words and write it in the brackets:

W H O S E . . . . (_____)

W O R S E . . . . (_____)

S O R R O W . . . . (_____)

H O R R O R . . . . (_____)

H O R S E . . . . (_____)

We are trying to match a digit to a letter. We are looking for a digit which is in the same position in the numbers as a letter in the words.

Always spend a few seconds studying carefully all the words and all the numbers.

Technique:

1. Write the words on top of the numbers on your paper, or vice versa, so you can look at them clearly.

2. Look for clues:

5681	5762	5761	8651	7651
∧	∧	∧		

HOSE	SHOE	ROSE	SORE	SHOW
	∧		∧	∧

Three numbers begin with *5*.
Three words begin with *S*.

3.   Match all the '5's to the letters 'S'.

HOSE	SHOE	ROSE	SORE	SHOW
5	*5*	*5*	*5*	*5*

4.   Now look for another clue. Try to be time-efficient.
      Try to find a clue that will be of the most benefit.
      For instance, can we work out the letter that corresponds to a 7?
      That would be most useful in distinguishing between 8651 and 7651.
      7 is the second digit in two of the numbers which begin with a 5.
      H is the second letter in two of the words which begin with S.
      So match *H* to 7.

HOSE	SHOE	ROSE	SORE	SHOW
7 5	*5 7*	*5*	*5*	*5 7*

We now know that *7651* is *HOSE*.

That is sufficient to work out the numerical value of each word.

5.   Complete.

HOSE	SHOE	ROSE	SORE	SHOW
7 6 5 1	*5 7 6 1*	*8 6 5 1*	*5 6 8 1*	*5 7 6 2*

6.   Check.
      Are all the E's a 1?   H's a 7?   O's a 6?   and so on.

7.   Answer the questions.

WHOSE is *27651*   *WORSE* is *26851*   *SORROW* is *568862*
HORROR is *768868*   and   *HORSE* is *76851*.

NOTE:

1. Always look for clues which will save you time. For example, there are often two identical letters in a word such as:

L O O K   or   S M I L E S

Look for a similar pattern in the digits.

2. Perhaps you can find the value of the 'odd' word - the one that is different from the others, for example:

L O A D	D O N E	L A N E
2 4 6 3	5 4 1 2	5 1 6 3

D O N E would be the best and most obvious to go for.

Two words begin with L and two numbers begin with 5.
These can be identified with the eye.
D O N E is the only word which begins with D and will match therefore to *2 4 6 3*.
From this, the numerical value of the other words can be found by speedy deduction.

3. Occasionally the numerical value for a letter is given in the instructions at the top of the question. DO NOT OVERLOOK IT.

4. Sometimes the examiner has quite deliberately placed two different letters into the same position in the words, and matched them to two different digits in the same position in the numbers. In this example:

MAIN	IDEA	NAME
3 7 1 4	5 4 2 1	2 4 3 5

Here, the M occupies the 1st and the 3rd positions in two of the words (MAIN and NAME). So does the letter I (IDEA and MAIN). The I is a 3, and the M is a 2. If, in error, I matched the I to the 2 and the M to the 3 it would not work out correctly and once realised I could waste valuable time trying to rectify it.

If the words do not fit perfectly with the numbers or symbols, GO BACK TO THE BEGINNING AND START AGAIN. This is more time-efficient than trying to correct the first mistake.

TYPE 33.2:

Symbols are often used instead of numbers but the procedure is exactly the same.

Match a symbol to a letter and each time fill in all the letters you can until one or more words become obvious.

You are allowed 30 seconds per question.

Now turn to the next page for Practice of these Types.

PRACTICE TYPE THIRTY-THREE

TYPE 33.1:

The following number codes 8435, 5368, 5436 and 8536 stand for TARS, SEAT, STAR and TEAR but not in the same order. Find the code for each of the following and write the answer in the brackets:

START........ (_____)

ARTS........ (_____)

STATE .... (_____)

SEATS .... (_____)

(**NOTE:** Take a few seconds to study the words carefully. For instance, there is a 'T' in each of the words. Is there a number that will match ? Alternatively there is 'EA' in two of the words.)

The words PEAR, REAP, SEAP and APES are coded 7519, 1957, 9514 and 4519 but not necessarily in that order. Write down the words for which the following stand:

9517......... (_____)

791457....... (_____)

79514 .... (_____)

(**NOTE:** Three of these words have 'EA' in the middle so can you find the value of 'APES' straight away? Alternatively, all the words have 'P' in them.)

6153, 5316, 5317 and 6317 are codes for the following words MEAL, LAME, LEAN and MEAN but not necessarily in that order. Write down the codes for the following:

NAME .... (_____)

MALE .... (_____)

MANE .... (_____)

ELM .... (_____)

(**NOTE:** Can you find the value of LAME straightaway ?)

The words **NOTE, BOUT, TONE, TUBE** and **BONE** are written 2465, 1465, 1325, 6415 and 2431 but not necessarily in that order. If the value of R is 7, find the code for each of the following and write your answers in the brackets.

TROUT . . . . (_____)

BONNET . . . . . . (_____)

BUTTON . . . . . . (_____)

Using the same code, what words do each of the following stand for?

251157 . . . . (_____)

74315 . . . . (_____)

742257 . . . . (_____)

3164, 4516, 3165, 1365 and 6135 are the codes for **CARE, RACE, ACRE, CART** and **TEAR** but not in the same order. Find the codes for each of the following and write your answers in the brackets.

CREATE . . . . . . (_____)

TRACE . . . . (_____)

TERRACE . . . . . (_____)

TYPE 33.2:

The following five words **TEAMS, STEAM, MATES, SEAMS** and **TAMES** are written below in code but not necessarily in the same order. The same code is used for all the words. Write in the brackets the correct word for each code.

! % ? £ @ . . (_____)

@ ! £ % ? . . (_____)

! £ % ? @ . . (_____)

? % ! £ @ . . (_____)

@ £ % ? @ . . (_____)

The following five words have been written in code below but not in the same order:

BEND   DEBT   BENT   TEND   DENT

Write in the brackets the correct word for each set of symbols:

      *   £ $ + ... (_____)

      O   £ $ + ... (_____)

      O   £ $ * . . . . (_____)

      +   £ $ * . . . . (_____)

      +   £   O   * . . . . (_____)

(**NOTE:** Which of these is 'DEBT' ? Four of these have 'EN' in the middle.)

Here are five words BOAT, TOAD, DATE, DOTE and BEAD. Below you will find these same words written in code with the same code used for all the questions. Write the word which stands for each of the code words in the brackets:

      ?   +   &   * . . . . (_____)

      @   &   *   ! . . . . (_____)

      *   +   &   @ . . . . (_____)

      @   +   *   ! . . . . (_____)

      ?   !   &   @ . . . . (_____)

NOTE, TONE, OPEN, PENT and NOON are written in code below, but not in the same order. The same code has been used for all the words. Write in the brackets the correct word for each code word.

      O   ÷   ÷   O . . . . (_____)

      #   *   O   £ . . . . (_____)

      O   ÷   £   * . . . . (_____)

      £   ÷   O   * . . . . (_____)

      ÷   #   *   O . . . . (_____)

TECHNIQUE TYPE THIRTY-FOUR

Type Thirty-Four below is one of the simplest Type of code question and is quite straightforward.

Here, one WORD and its CODE word are given. Often two words and their code words are given. Occasionally number codes are given instead of letter codes.

Using the letters of the code word, you are asked to translate words into code, and code into words.

Example:

In a secret code M Y F Z A S D S V T X Y V stands for C O M P R E H E N S I O N. Using the same code, work out how the following words would be written:

C O M P O S E . . . .   (_____)

P R I S M . . . .   (_____)

C O M M O N . . . .   (_____)

E R R O R . . . .   (_____)

What do the following code words stand for?

T D X V S . . . .   (_____)

Z D Y V S . . . .   (_____)

M D X F S . . . .   (_____)

Technique:

1. Firstly, set out the CODE word above the proper WORD as below.
    Draw distinct columns for the letters.

Code	M	Y	F	Z	A	S	D	S	V	T	X	Y	V
Word	C	O	M	P	R	E	H	E	N	S	I	O	N

2. Spread out the CODE word so it is quite clear to which WORD letter each code letter belongs. Do not cause unnecessary confusion by writing the letters and words too closely together.

3. Write alongside each set of letters which is the CODE and which is the WORD. Write 'CODE' and 'WORD' appropriately as shown above.

4. If you are given a CODE word your finger will move along the top row of letters labelled 'CODE'.

   If you are given a proper WORD to translate into code, your finger should move along those letters opposite 'WORD'.
   It is important there can be no confusion.

Let us work through this Example together:

You are asked to write the word COMPOSE in code.

Technique:

1. Moving along the row of letters labelled 'WORD', stop at the letter C.
   The CODE letter above C is M. Write down *M*.
   Now move onto the letter O in COMPOSE.

2. Again, moving along the row of letters labelled 'WORD', stop at the letter O.
   The CODE letter above O is Y. Write down *Y*.
   Now move on to the letter M of COMPOSE.

3. The CODE letter above M is F. Write down *F*, and so on.

In this way, taking care, you should be able to correctly recognise the CODE words for :

C O M P O S E . . . . (*M Y F Z Y T S*)

P R I S M . . . . (*Z A X T F*)

C O M M O N . . . . (*M Y F F Y V*)

E R R O R . . . . (*S A A Y A*)

You are now asked for the WORDS for T D X V S, Z D Y V S and M D X F S.

You identify the proper WORDS from these codes in exactly the same way as above, except this time your finger should move along the row of letters labelled 'CODE'. In this way, you will translate, letter by letter, the CODE word given into a proper WORD.

4.   Moving along the row of letters labelled 'CODE', find the letter T.
        Below CODE letter T is the letter S. Write down *S*.

5.   In the same way, find the CODE letter for D.
        Below CODE letter D is the letter H. Write down *H*, and so on.

Again, with care, you should be able to identify the words :

            T D X V S . . . .   (_*S H I N E*_)

            Z D Y V S . . . .   (_*P H O N E*_)

            M D X F S . . . .   (_*C H I M E*_)

The time allowed here is 30 seconds per word/code. Three-and-a-half minutes
then, would be allowed for this seven-part question.

NOTE:
It is usual for an identical letter to be used in both the CODE word and the
proper WORD. In this Example, for instance, S and M are found in both the
CODE word and the proper WORD. Easy marks can be lost by carelessly
travelling along the wrong row of letters. That is why it is so very important to
remember to label the rows of letters 'CODE' and 'WORD' (never 'C' and 'W').
Do not overlook this. Mistakes made are likely to be this silly one.
Otherwise these codes are easy, quick and fun to do. Enjoy them!

You are allowed 30 seconds per question.

Now turn to the next page for Practice of this Type.

PRACTICE TYPE THIRTY-FOUR

In the following questions you will need to use the same code to find the answers. The code X P B S Y Q W O stands for C U R T A I N S and D Y O V M S stands for B A S K E T. Write the code for the following words :

ICESKATER............. (_____)

SUSTAIN .... (_____)

TAKE CARE .... (_____)

Using the same code write the words which the following code words stand for :

SYOVO .... (_____)

BYQOQW .... (_____)

DYOQW .... (_____)

SBYQWO .... (_____)

In a secret code X N W B X L V O B stands for T I M E T A B L E. Using the same code work out how the following words would be written :

METAL .... (_____)

BELT .... (_____)

MEALTIME.............. (_____)

Using the same code, decipher what the following code words stand for :

VBLX .... (_____)

OLXB .... (_____)

In the following code questions you need to use two code words to find the answers. S X O M Z S D X stands for B E N D A B L E and Y N N Y O X O Q stands for I M M I N E N T .
Using the same codes, how would you write the following words?

L A D E N . . . . (_____)

M A L L E A B L E . . . . (_____)

A N I M A L . . . . (_____)

T A B L E T . . . . (_____)

Using the same code write the words which the following code words stand for:

M Z S S D X . . . . (_____)

N X M M D X . . . . (_____)

N Z O M Z Q X . . . . (_____)

N Y D Y Q Z O Q . . . . (_____)

_____

In a secret code W S T B V R O T M V Z S T stands for C O N S T E R N A T I O N . Using the same code work out how the following words should be written:

S T R I C T . . . . (_____)

C E N T R E . . . . (_____)

T E R R O R . . . . (_____)

E R A S E R . . . . (_____)

Using the same code what do the following code words say?

V O M W V S O . . . . (_____)

T R M V R O . . . . (_____)

W S T V O M W V . . . . (_____)

_____

In the following questions V K R W S P Q M T J P I stands for R E L A T I O N S H I P. Using this code, how would you write the following words?

P L A N E T .... (_____)

R E S H A P E .... (_____)

L E A S H .... (_____)

P O L I T E .... (_____)

Using the same code, what words do the following stand for?

S V W P M .... (_____)

S V W M T I Q V S .... (_____)

R K T T Q M .... (_____)

In the following code question T R A F F I C is written F C Z X X R M. Using this code, how would you write the following words?

C I T R I C .... (_____)

A T T R A C T .... (_____)

C R A F T .... (_____)

R I F F R A F F .... (_____)

Using the same code, what do the following stand for?

X Z M F .... (_____)

F Z C R X X .... (_____)

TECHNIQUE TYPE THIRTY-FIVE

These codes are not difficult.

You must simply substitute numbers for letters and calculate the value of the equations you are given.

Example:

If A = 6, B = 5, C = 4, D = 3 and E = 2, what is the value of the following?

A + C – B   Give your answer as a LETTER . . . .(_____)

$$\frac{A + C}{E}$$ Give your answer as a LETTER . . . .(_____)

If all the letters of B A D were multiplied together and the answer divided by E, what would be the answer written as a NUMBER? . . . . (_____)

Technique:

Simply substitute the correct number for each letter, and calculate.
Here:

6 + 4 – 5 = 5   written as a LETTER . . . . (_B_)

$$\frac{6 + 4}{2} = 5$$ written as a LETTER . . . . (_B_)

B x A x D = 5 x 6 x 3 = 90
90 ÷ E (2) = 45   written as a NUMBER . . . . (_45_)

NOTE:

1. Sometimes you are asked to give your answer as a LETTER, and sometimes as a NUMBER. You can easily lose marks here by making careless errors. Be sure you know which you are being asked for. Check with each part of the question. (What you are being asked for is usually given in CAPITAL LETTERS in the instructions. You must take care to read the question carefully.)

2. When one letter or number is written on top of another letter or number, you must DIVIDE the bottom number into the top.

3. Be sure to know the meaning of the following terms which often occur in this Type of code question:

'Product of'	means multiply together
'Difference between'	means subtract
'Sum of'	means add together

You are allowed 30 seconds per question.

Now turn to the next page for Practice of this Type.

PRACTICE TYPE THIRTY-FIVE

If D = 5, E = 1, F = 8, I = 3, R = 6 what is the value of the following? Underline the correct answer in the brackets:

Which is greater? $\left\{ \dfrac{F + E}{I}, \ F - E + D, \ (R - E) \times D \right\}$

What does $(F \times I + R) \times D$ equal?............ (70, 100, 150, 120)

Give the answer of the following as a NUMBER:

$F \times I + D$ .... (_____)

$(E + R) \times I$................ (_____)

$D + F - E$.................. (_____)

Give the answer of the following as a LETTER:

$\dfrac{F + I + E}{2}$ .... (_____)

$\dfrac{(R \times F) + (2 \times E)}{10}$ ...... (_____)

In each of the following questions:

S = 1,   E = 4,   D = 5,   K = 8

Add E to S and divide the answer by D. Give your answer as a LETTER.
(_____)

Multiply together the letters D S K and divide your answer by E. Give your answer as a NUMBER .... (_____)

Subtract D from K and multiply the answer by E. Write your answer as a NUMBER...................................... (_____)

Total all the letters E S D and divide the answer by the product of S and D. Write your answer as a NUMBER .... (_____)

From the difference between K and S subtract the sum of D and S. Give your answer as a LETTER.................................... (_____)

If B = 6, A = 3, C = 4, D = 9 and E = 5 what is the value of the following?

$$\frac{B + C + E}{A}$$ Write your answer as a LETTER . . (____)

$$\frac{(B - C) \times D}{A}$$ Write your answer as a LETTER . . (____)

$$\frac{A \times E \times C}{D + E - C}$$ Write your answer as a LETTER . . (____)

Find the difference between the product of B and D and the sum of B and A.
Write your answer as a NUMBER . . . . (____)

From the total of BEAD subtract the product of A and E and divide your answer by C. Write your answer as a NUMBER . . . . (____)

Find the difference between the sum of D and E and the product of D and E.
Write your answer as a NUMBER . . . . (____)

From the sum of D and B subtract the product of A and C.
Write your answer as a LETTER . . . . (____)

In each of the following questions:

$$M = 9 \quad N = 7 \quad O = 5 \quad P = 4 \quad Q = 1$$

Now find the value of the following:

$$\frac{N \times O + Q}{M}$$ Write your answer as a LETTER . . (____)

$$\frac{M + N \times Q}{P}$$ Write your answer as a LETTER . . (____)

$$\frac{M \times P - Q}{N}$$ Write your answer as a LETTER . . (____)

From the product of N and M subtract the difference between the sum of N and O and the product of P and Q. Divide your answer by O.
Write your answer as a NUMBER . . . . (____)

If J = 6, M = 3, S = 4, A = 2 and E = 5, find the value of the following.
Write your answers in the brackets.

$$\frac{J + S + A}{M}$$ Write your answer as a LETTER . . (____)

$$\frac{M \times S \times 2}{J}$$ Write your answer as a LETTER . . (____)

$$\frac{E \times A + J}{S}$$ Write your answer as a LETTER . . (____)

$(J + S) \times A + E$ Write your answer as a NUMBER . . (____)

Which TWO letters give J as their product? . . . . (_____)

Which TWO letters give E as their sum? . . . . (_____)

If the product of J and A is greater than the sum of E and M write X, unless the
difference between the product of J and A and the sum of E and M is greater than
E in which case write Y . . . . (____)

PRIZE CERTIFICATE

Pupil's Name: ....

This is to certify that the above-named pupil has completed the Practice Exercises in Verbal Reasoning Technique and Practice 4 and has achieved:

a BEST SCORE of .... within the time allowed.

I .... (Parent)

am extremely proud of these achievements and undertake to

(insert details of Special Award) ....

....

....

in recognition of this achievement and to show my appreciation of all the hard work and effort that has gone into doing so well.

Well Done!
Congratulations!

ADDITIONAL EXERCISES

Additional exercises to improve your child's speed and accuracy.

A.   To improve ability to listen to instructions and carry them out quickly and accurately.

Take any story book, and ask your child to find certain things in it, for instance:

a.   What is the third word on the fourth line on page 15?

b.   How many letters are in the last word on the bottom of page 16?

c.   How many vowels are there in the seventh word on the fourteenth line of page 10?

d.   How many a's are there in the sixth word on the ninth line on page 7, and so on.

B.   To improve your child's ability to work through the alphabet quickly and accurately.

Take a dictionary and ask your child to open the page at the letter 'M', 'N', 'B' and so on, so he learns to judge the position of the letters in the alphabet and is able to estimate where to open the dictionary to find a particular letter.

C.   To give your child a concept of 30 seconds and so be able to pace himself in an examination that requires him to answer one question in 30 seconds.

a.   While checking with your own watch ask your child to tell you when he thinks 30 seconds has passed. Repeat until he can judge it accurately within 5 seconds either side.

b.   'Speed handwriting' - see how many times he can write his name in 30 seconds. Try again. Can he improve his 'record'? Many children I have taught can achieve up to 30 five-letter words in 30 seconds!

> TRY TO AWAKEN YOUR CHILD'S INNATE SPEED
> WHILE MAINTAINING ACCURACY.

PERSONAL RECORD TABLE

Name: ....

DATE	TYPE	No.of Qs	SCORE	MAX. TIME	ACTUAL TIME	COMMENTS
	31	8		4		
	32.1	8		4		
	32.2	8		4		
	32.3	8		4		
	32.4	8		4		
	32.1 - 32.4	20		10		
	33.1	20		10		
	33.2	20		10		
	34	40		20		
	35	30		15		

How to fill in the PERSONAL RECORD TABLE:

The parent should fill in the Date of the test in Column 1.
What is your child's score? Enter in Column 4.
Enter your child's Actual Time in Column 6.
Do you need to make a note of anything ?
Could your child do with more practice ?
Was his score high enough ?
There are more Practice Exercises of all these Types in Verbal Reasoning Further Practice Exercises.
What about your child's time?   Is that: Good?   Bad?   Getting better?
Record your Comments in Column 7.

ANSWERS

TYPE THIRTY-ONE:

c
d
d
b
c
b
b
d

TYPE THIRTY-TWO:

Type 32.1:

STOP
AMLC
MQICQ
FLAME
FISH
GREEN (D)
BLMS
TDEL

Type 32.2:

HATE
VAN
YLLP
HGZTV
HIT
ORW
HURT
DRGS

Type 32.3:

MAN
LEAF
21 19 22 15 12
CCNFF
C 16 O 5 B 19
DEAR
BOOT
Z 1 W 5 U

Type 32.4:

HEAD
WWAIIT
EERADD
STTEMM
FED
ROE
PIG
CCATT

Types 32.1 - 32.4:

GIRL
RULER
4 X 19 Q
CCNFF
TXRYAZY
PACK
BENCH
O 10 U 4 G
YAABCCHDT
MVHG
STILL
CLOUD
15 12 9 22 5
MUKRL
MUG
BIRD
FAABCCED
5 C 9 G
SLLU
BULB

TYPE THIRTY-THREE:

Type 33.1:

85365	BETTER
3658	ROUTE
85354	ROBBER
84358	
	365145
PEAS	46135
SPARES	4566135
SPEAR	
7153	
5163	
5173	**Type 33.2:**
365	TAMES
	STEAM
17431	TEAMS
246651	MATES
231146	SEAMS

TEND
BEND
BENT
DENT
DEBT

BOAT
DATE
TOAD
DOTE
BEAD

NOON
PENT
NOTE
TONE
OPEN

TYPE THIRTY-FOUR:

QXMOVYSMB
OPOSYQW
SYVM XYBM
TASKS
RAISIN
BASIN
TRAINS
WBXLO
VBOX
WBLOXNWB
BEAT
LATE
DZMXO
NZDDXZSDX
ZOYNZD
QZSDXQ
DABBLE
MEDDLE
MANDATE
MILITANT

BVOZWV
WRTVOR
VROOSO
ROMBRO
TRACTOR
NEATER
CONTRACT
IRWMKS
VKTJWIK
RKWTJ
IQRPSK
TRAIN
TRANSPORT
LESSON
MRFCRM
ZFFCZMF
MCZXF
CRXXCZXX
FACT
TARIFF

TYPE THIRTY-FIVE:

(R – E) x D
150
29
21
12
R
D

S
10
12
2
S

E
B
B
45
2
31

A

P
P
O
11

S
S
S
25
A x M or M x A
A + M or M + A
X